THANK YOU
FOR THE MUSIC

Published in 2022 by OH!
An Imprint of Welbeck Non-Fiction Limited,
part of Welbeck Publishing Group.
Based in London and Sydney.
www.welbeckpublishing.com

Compilation text © Welbeck Non-Fiction Limited 2022
Design © Welbeck Non-Fiction Limited 2022

ISBN 978-1-80069-232-9

Project manager: Russell Porter
Compilation and layout: RH
Production: Jess Brisley

A CIP catalogue record for this book is available from the British Library

Printed in China

10 9 8 7 6 5 4 3 2 1

Illustration: Original photograph by Michael Ochs Archives/Getty Images

THANK YOU FOR THE MUSIC

THE LITTLE GUIDE TO

ABBA

CONTENTS

INTRODUCTION

Abba blasted their way onto the global pop scene with a Eurovision Song Contest win in 1974, although they had all been heavily involved in music professionally long before that. The song, "Waterloo" – Abba's tenth single in Sweden – was a top-10 hit around the world and spurred them on to enormous chart success with singles, then albums, then compilations selling in the millions.

They truly conquered the world for years, recording, touring, performing and entertaining huge crowds everywhere they went. They were one of the first non-English-speaking groups to enjoy such success. But after less than a decade, the dream was fading, the divorces final, and the four went their separate ways, seemingly never to record together again. Superstardom was over, but their music stayed popular and in every decade that passed, the question was asked: "Will Abba re-form?"

The answer was always no – they even allegedly turned down a billion-dollar tour – until the late 2010s, when rumours abounded and, finally, to enormous global fanfare, Abba revealed that a new 10-track album would be released in November 2021 and "virtual avatar" concerts would take place from May 2022: fans went wild.

This book remembers everything the super Swedish pop group represents: brilliant pop music, dynamic performances, the ultimate in 70s style, long-lasting influence and an enduring legacy. We have witty, honest and poignant quotes by and about Agnetha, Benny, Björn and Anni-Frid (better known by her nickname Frida), as well as words of wisdom from prominent fans and commentators alongside fun facts and stats.

This is a joyful celebration of the Swedish foursome and their incredible songs that conquered the world and still fill dancefloors today: We say thank you for the music!

CHAPTER
ONE

BECOMING
ABBA

The early careers of the four
musicians, singers and performers
that wowed the world:
Anni-Frid (Frida), Benny, Björn
and Agnetha.

I had a dream and it was fulfilled by meeting with Benny, Björn and Agnetha.

"

Anni-Frid

Abba formed in Stockholm in

1972

when the two couples
(Agnetha & Björn, Anni-Frid &
Benny) got together to sing and
play some music.

Benny was a member of the Hep
Stars, Björn was in the Hootenanny
Singers, and they had known each
other for a while.

> **"**
>
> I had a number one, yes, I was just 18 years old. So that was a good start. That was '68. **"**

Agnetha, *interview with Carol Vorderman on Loose Women, 2013.*

Source: youtube.com

From the little town where I come from, we came into the big city by train. I was very nervous and excited about making a record and it was a great moment for me.

Agnetha, 2004.

Source: abba-intermezzo.de

"

I never had any other plans.
As a seven-year-old I knew that it
was a singer I was going to be. "

Anni-Frid, *1973.*

Source: en.newsner.com

The quartet's first record
was "Hej, gamle man", a song
about an old Salvation Army
soldier, in

1970

It translates as
"Hello, old man" in English, and
was a B-side.

66

For one song we asked our wives
to come in for backing vocals
and all of a sudden, wow. They
sound good, we don't!

99

Benny, *interview with Adrian Lobb,*
The Big Issue, 2017.

Source: bigissue.com

"

I didn't occur to us that maybe
we should form a band until three
years [later]… in 1972.

"

Benny, *interview with David Morales, 2018.*

Source: backstageol.com

Not at first, no. But, like I say, the Beatles were around, so I saw what could be done and I decided to try.

Benny, on starting to write songs, interview with David Roberts for MBW's World's Greatest Songwriters.

Source: musicbusinessworldwide.com

Abba is also the name of a famous
fish-canning company in Sweden.
The band had to get permission
from The Abba Seafood Company
to use it.

Source: dn.se

We could feel that we clicked, but we had no idea that it would become the cooperation it became.

*Björn, on meeting Benny,
interview with Anna Bodin in Dagens Nyheter,
2020.*

Source: dn.se

"

The music scene changed with us – something like Abba didn't exist before; pop like that was not invented yet.

"

Anni-Frid, The Guardian, *2014.*

Source: theguardian.com

We should write a pop song in English, and see what happens.

Benny, *interview with David Morales, 2018.*

Source: backstageol.com

"

The energy exchange between us on stage and the audience was absolutely amazing.

"

Anni-Frid, *interview with Neil McMahon,*
Sydney Morning Herald, 2017.

I was shocked. I cried tears
of joy.

Agneta, *(as she was known then), on her
first song in the charts,* Jönköpingsposten,
1968.

Source: agnethaarchives.com

Agnetha was a telephonist
for a car firm while performing
with a local dance band...
The band proved popular, and
she had to choose between her
job and her musical career.

Source: smoothradio.com

As soon as Frida and Agnetha start singing, that's when it sounds Abba.

Benny, *on Abba's new music,* Chess *revival press night, 2018.*

Source: bbc.co.uk

"

You can imagine – you go to Brighton, and you are this band which is very well-known in Sweden but not outside. And bam! One night, and it all opens up.

"

Björn, *interview with Fred Bronson, Billboard, 1999.*

Source: abbaomnibus.net

Benny and I have worked together since 1966. We've had our fall-outs but never anything really serious and we don't see each other every day.

Björn, The Blackpool Gazette, _2014._

Source: icethesite.com

Björn and Benny's first song
together was called
"It Isn't Easy to Say" and was
recorded in 1966.

Source: thisdayinmusic.com

CHAPTER
TWO

ARRIVAL

It was a case of third time lucky for Abba at Sweden's Eurovision selection show, *Melodifestivalen*.

Abba made it through to represent their country, and they travelled to Brighton in England...

"

We had no idea that we could win this [Eurovision]. It came as a big surprise.

"

Agnetha, *interview with Carol Vorderman on* Loose Women, *2013.*

Source: youtube.com

Eurovision's winner for

1974

"Waterloo"
was a number-one hit in nine
countries. It was voted the best
ever Eurovision song at the event's
50th anniversary in 2005.

Source: scandipop.co.uk

… to make people realize us guys from the North Pole exist, we decided to enter the Eurovision Song Contest.

Benny, *interview with Adrian Lobb, The Big Issue, 2017.*

Source: bigissue.com

66

No… Well, actually I had a £20 bet on it, in Brighton, at 20–1. There were some good songs, but I did think ours was better.

99

Benny, *on Eurovision, interview with David Roberts for MBW's World's Greatest Songwriters.*

Source: musicbusinessworldwide.com

In the 70s, no one would admit that they liked Abba. The snobbery of the time wouldn't allow it.

Brian Eno, *interview with Paul Morley in The Observer, 2010.*

Source: stuff.co.nz

Benny and Anni-Frid
married in

1978

without telling
anyone – including Björn and
Agnetha.

Abba and me, we were the 70s.

Demis Roussos, The Times, *2015.*

Source: thetimes.co.uk

66

When I was eight, my pals and
I went up to my bedroom, put on
our party frocks and mimed to
Abba records using broom handles
as microphones. **99**

Kylie Minogue

Yes, the Australian tour was the most incredible of all the things that I experienced with Abba.

Agnetha

Source: *As I Am: Abba Before & Beyond* by Agnetha Fältskog with Brita Åhman, Virgin Books, 1997

"

When everything is truthful and falls into place in the way that our music did, even though we were not really aware of it then – then that music will have a power and energy that will not expire but which will live on in many different ways.

"

Anni-Frid, *interview with Georg Cederskog, Dagens Nyheter, 2010.*

Source: icethesite.com

66

There were times that were a bit,
how shall I say, strained.

99

Agnetha, *on the early years, interview*
with Carol Vorderman on Loose Women, *2013.*

Source: youtube.com

"

We opened with a traditional Swedish folk song because we thought it would connect with the Irish. You love your folk songs and there's that link with us.

"

Benny, *on Abba's only concert in Ireland, interview in the* Belfast Telegraph, *2017.*

Source: belfasttelgraph.co.uk

Well we were at home a lot so they would have had to come to our houses and knock on our doors to offer us drugs!

Anni-Frid, *on clean living with Abba,*
The Guardian, *2014.*

Source: theguardian.com

"

Pop-star glamour, we're all totally unimpressed by that, but to be creative in the studio, that's something else, just to be us, just to try things and see what it sounds like.

"

Björn, *interview with Zane Lowe,*
Apple Music, 2021.

Source: nme.com

66

We have met the enemy and they are them.

99

Robert Christgau, *on Abba, 1979.*

Source: npr.org

66

Abba's image was original and contemporary for the time. It was cutting edge, although it's hard to appreciate that now. They were true original musicians.

99

Kim Wilde, Let's Talk About Abba
by Stany Van Wymeersch, International Abba Fan Club magazine.

Source: abbafanclub.nl

Insane.

Björn, *on Abba's history.*

Source: pressreader.com

In

1980

there were approximately
3.5 million applications
for 12,000 tickets for an Abba
concert at London's Royal Albert
Hall – enough to fill the venue
580 times.

Source: memories.royalalberthall.com

66

Oh I am not a performer,
I'm a songwriter.

99

Benny, *interview with David Roberts*
for MBW's World's Greatest Songwriters.

Source: musicbusinessworldwide.com

"

I swear to you, none of us know why it brings happiness to a lot of people. That's what I call a miracle!

"

Björn, on the effect of Abba's music, interview with William J. Connolly in Gay Times.

Source: gaytimes.co.uk

66

We don't want to write political songs. We don't want to turn our records into speeches.

99

Benny, *to Mick Farren, NME, 1976.*

Source: rocksbackpages.com

When Abba performed
"Waterloo" – the song that won
the Eurovision Song Contest –
the UK awarded it

points.

Source: memories.royalalberthall.com

Because it's kind of strange they would give us zero points.
It sounds like they were trying to do something cunning.

__Björn__, on the UK awarding "nul points" for "Waterloo", BBC Breakfast, 2021.

Source: bbc.co.uk

"

I wasn't a big fan of Abba in the 70s, Benny took the girls and used them like instruments.

"

Cher, The New York Times, *2018*.

Source: etonline.com

> 66
>
> The girls do, but Benny and me don't have time for that. 99

Björn, *on stage fright*, Bravo, *1977*.

Source: abbaarticles.blogspot.com

In Sydney, Australia in

1977

fans queued for 24 hours
to get into an Abba concert with
non-numbered seating.

What a fantastic public.
They are quite incredible here
in Copenhagen!

Björn, 1977.

"

Abba's richly textured renderings of seemingly straightforward hooks were the aural equivalent of Dolly Parton's axiom: 'It costs a lot of money to look this cheap.'

"

Barry Walters, *"Abba's Essential, Influential Melody"*, 2015.

Source: npr.org

Abba's setlist from
the

70s

often included
a "mini-musical" entitled
"The Girl With the Golden Hair".

It was included on
ABBA: The Album.

"

OK, so we're not big in America.
We don't care. We don't want
to go.

"

Björn, *interview with Fred Bronson,*
Billboard, 1999.

Source: abbaomnibus.net

KEEP BRITAIN TIDY

T-shirts worn by Abba, 1977.

"

What Made Australians the World's Most Feverish Abba Fans?

Neil McMahon, *headline in* The Sydney Morning Herald, *2017.*

Source: smh.com.au

"

In all the world except America (which was too busy celebrating centennials and electing presidents) – 1976 was the Year of Abba.

Simon Frith, *Creem, 1977.*

Source: rocksbackpages.com

66

The world's most beautiful people
[Abba] don't sweat!

99

Bosse Norling, *Abba's tour leader,*
Interview with Lars Petterson, New Zealand
Women's Weekly, *1977.*

ARRIVAL

In

1976

a "Get Abba to Brisbane"
petition had managed to muster
over 30,000 signatures.

Brisbane Telegraph, 1976.

"

Okay, I know Abba don't sound anything like either Motown or Philles. They aren't funky, they have no soul and they're bland to the point of making baby food seem raunchy.

"

Mick Farren, NME, 1976.

Source: rocksbackpages.com

In those days, you didn't even make any money touring. Production was so expensive [with] a lot of people and stuff.
And apart from the time you're on stage, the rest is utterly, utterly boring and unproductive.

Björn, The Weekend Australian, *2007*.

Abba's rider in 1977 included:
Johnnie Walker black label
whiskey, Pommery champagne,
soda water, Coca-Cola, coffee, tea,
milk and fresh fruit.

CHAPTER

THREE

SUPER TROUPER

They had the world at their feet: international tours, top-selling music and constant adoration.

But it was not to last...

I can spot empty flattery and know exactly where I stand. In the end it's really only my own approval or disapproval that means anything.

Agnetha

"

We don't plan in advance what we are going to do. We just go to our island and record whatever's in our heads.

Benny, *to Mick Farren*, NME, 1976.

Source: rocksbackpages.com

At their commercial zenith in the late 70s Abba were reputedly second only to Volvo in their contribution to Sweden's exports.

Andrew Harrison, *2014.*

Source: bbc.com

66

I wake up quite early and the first job is a coffee. I have up to 20 cups a day – black with a dash of milk.

99

Bjorn, *interview with Emma Broomfield,* The Sunday Times, *2020.*

Source: thetimes.co.uk

You're not really supposed to like
Abba in Sweden. It's nerdy. **99**

Izabella Scorupco

"

Pervasive airplay might transform
what is now a nagging annoyance
into an aural totem. **"**

Robert Christgau, *on Abba,*
Village Voice, 1976.

Source: npr.org

It becomes pretty evident when you research the newspaper and magazine articles devoted to Abba and Agnetha from the 1970s onwards that she and the band had a love–hate relationship with the Swedish press.

Daniel Ward, *author of* Agnetha Faltskog: The Girl with the Golden Hair, *interview, 2016.*

Source: abbafansblog.blogspot.com

A NON
SMOKING
GENERATION

T-shirts worn by Agnetha, 1980.

But mostly it's very nice.
Sometimes someone comes
close, when I'm in a restaurant,
asking for an autograph.
But that's no problem. Nothing
to worry about.

Agnetha, *on being recognized in public,
interviewed by Lasse Bengtsson, 2004.*

Source: abba-intermezzo.de

66

I have no idea why Abba's music is still so popular. 99

Benny, *interview with Adrian Lobb,*
The Big Issue, *2017.*

Source: bigissue.com

Things were happening in real life too, not just in [our] working life. [Anni-Frid Lyngstad and I] got divorced, [Björn Ulvaeus and Agnetha Fältskog] got divorced. At first we still worked together though because we knew what we had.

Benny, *interview on* Lorraine, *ITV, 2017.*

Source: digitalspy.com

" There's a real melancholy in [Abba's] songs… all the flourishes, like big double octaves on the piano. We stole them like crazy. "

Elvis Costello

> **"**
>
> *ABBA: The Movie*; I got a lot of grief for working on that. **"**

Lasse Hallström

Source: brainyquote.com

The director of most of Abba's videos – and *ABBA: The Movie* – was Oscar-winning movie maker Lasse Hallström.

Björn wrote it about us after the breakdown of our marriage.
The fact he wrote it exactly when we divorced is touching really.

Agnetha, *on "The Winner Takes It All",* Evening Standard.

Source: alvipp.com

"

It is the experience of a divorce,
but it's fiction.

"

*Björn, on "The Winner Takes It All", interview
with Craig McLean, The Observer, 2008.*

Source: theguardian.com

I liked Abba when they weren't fashionable, you know? I never deserted Abba. I genuinely think their music is extraordinary.

Michael Ball, Chess *revival press night, 2018.*

Source: bbc.co.uk

I was shocked by some of the on-stage chat though, which seems all this time later to be so corny and contrived.

Ludvig Andersson *(Benny's son), on the concert recordings, 2019.*

Source: icethesite.com

Yes, a lot, especially when I began to write my own lyrics. I don't like many of them any more.

Agnetha, *upon being asked whether she has always been critical of herself and her songs, interview with Lasse Bengtsson, 2004.*

Source: abba-intermezzo.de

Abba have sold
more records than Bruce
Springsteen, Metallica and
Fleetwood Mac.

Source: wikipedia.org

We felt like we had something so valuable in the group that, even though it was difficult, we didn't want to break that up. And to prove it, we did some of our best stuff after that.

Benny, *on divorce and continuing with Abba, 2017.*

Source: express.co.uk

Abba's performance of
"Thank You For the Music"
on the *Late Late Breakfast
Show* in

1982

was the last time
they performed together for
four decades.

There was a period after Abba that was too much to take.

Agnetha, interview in The Sun, *2004*.

Source: thesun.co.uk

"

I don't buy pastries and other things that I love. And I don't drink alcohol so I can't celebrate with that. And I don't smoke.

"

Björn, *interview with Anna Bodin in* Dagens Nyheter, *2020.*

Source: dn.se

The press has always written that I am a recluse and a mysterious woman, but I am more down-to-earth than they think.

Agnetha, *interview with Moira Petty, Daily Mail, 2013.*

Source: dailymail.co.uk

Abba recorded an album in 1980, entitled *Gracias Por La Música*.

It featured 10 of their hits sung in Spanish, including "Reina Danzante" ("Dancing Queen") and "Conociéndome, Conociéndote" ("Knowing Me, Knowing You").

A divorce is something terrible to go through. But it's even worse to be subjected to the tabloids, lies in articles where they present them as the truth.

Agnetha, *interview in* VeckoRevyn, *1979.*

Source: agnetha-love.tumblr.com

❝

I think Abba have a pure joy to their music and that's what makes them extraordinary.

❞

Bono

'The Day Before You Came' is the most underestimated Abba song of all time. The lyric is unreal, and these guys did not speak English as their natural language.

Pete Waterman, Let's Talk About Abba by Stany Van Wymeersch, International Abba Fan Club magazine.

Source: abbafanclub.nl

66

I can't listen to that song too much
because it can make me cry if I'm
in a vulnerable mood.

99

Jarvis Cocker, on *"The Day Before
You Came"*, article by Louise Brailey in Crack,
2018.

Source: crackmagazine.net

People should get up and dance, that's what *Mamma Mia!* does with you.

Björn, The Blackpool Gazette, *2014*.

Source icethesite.com

ABBA Gold
is the #2 bestselling album
of all time in the UK, beating
The Beatles and Adele.

CHAPTER
FOUR

SO LONG

The band played their
last concert and recorded
their last music,
although there was never an
official announcement.

For 40 years the question about
a reunion was asked...

Never in our wildest dreams did we think that these songs we wrote would last for such a long time.

Benny, *Reuters, 2018.*

"

We will never appear on
stage again.

"

Björn, *The* Daily Telegraph, *2008.*

It's important to take care of my own business now that Abba has disbanded.

Agnetha, Svenska Dagbladet, *1984.*

Source: agnethaarchives.com

Anni-Frid's first post-Abba
solo album was produced
by Phil Collins.

It was released in

1982

Maybe I was a recluse for some years. I was so tired once Abba was over and just wanted to be calm and with my children.

Agnetha, *interview with Moira Petty,*
Daily Mail, 2013.

Source: dailymail.co.uk

"

[A reunion] is the inevitable question. No, we wouldn't.

Björn, *BBC, 2013.*

Source: smh.com.au

Bjorn and I had separated and I had torn myself away from the children. I just wanted to go home, home, home.

Agnetha, Daily Express, *2021*

ABBA Gold
has sold more than

30m

copies
around the world.

We do speak – it happens. Just not very often. Whenever I don't turn up at an Abba event people assume we don't speak.

Agnetha, *interview in* The Sun, *2004.*

Source: thesun.co.uk

I hate flying. This time I came all the way from Sweden by bus and boat.

Agnetha, *on foreign travel (to Amsterdam), 1983.*

Source: abbaarticles.blogspot.com

We don't have any plans to work
together again.

Agnetha, *interview in* The Sun, *2004.*

Source: thesun.co.uk

"

Yeah, why not. I don't know if the girls sing anything anymore.

"

Benny, *on a reunion, 2010.*

We found out quite early that 'Dancing Queen' had become an anthem and we were very proud that we've been chosen by the community. **99**

Bjorn, *interview with William J. Connolly in* Gay Times.

Source: gaytimes.co.uk

" That's the downside of racing.
But I've been around for a while,
and it's always best to remember
that the most common thing
in racing is that your horse
doesn't win. "

Benny, *on horse racing,*
interview with Howard Wright in Horse Racing:
I Have A Dream.

Source: thefreelibrary.com

It goes from generation to generation… It's such a good energy.

Agnetha, on Abba's influence on a new generation of artists, interview with Carol Vorderman on Loose Women, 2013.

Source: youtube.com

We said no because they wanted 250 shows or something, it was incredible. No chance! No chance.

Agnetha, *on the rumoured $1bn reunion tour,* Radio Times.

I could see us doing something together in the future. It is just a feeling I have that it would be fun to get together, talk a bit about the past and maybe perform together.

Agnetha, *on a reunion, 2011.*

66

I suspect it could be 'love', despite its drawbacks in the rhyming department.

99

Björn, on his favourite word, interview with Rosanna Greenstreet, The Guardian, 2020.

Source: theguardian.com

We've had ridiculous offers for just one television show. We just say no. If we were to come back – which is not going to happen – the motivation has to be something completely different from money.

Bjorn, *interview with Fred Bronson,* Billboard, *1999.*

Source: abbaomnibus.net

"

I remember Tim [Rice] telling me that he had an idea for a musical and he said to me that he was hoping that Abba would be writing the music, which I thought was a pretty wild idea because they were obviously known very much as pop writers.

"

Elaine Page

I've always liked Abba and saw the original *Mamma Mia!* musical on Broadway three times. 99

***Cher**, press release, 2018.*

Source: etonline.com

66

… so many of their songs contain snapshots of what it means to be human and have a human experience, which makes it instantly relatable.

99

John Grant, *article by Louise Brailey in Crack, 2018.*

Source: crackmagazine.net

We're a bit older now and have our minor ailments. We struggle on. But I don't dare say, because it's a bit uncertain.

Agnetha, *2021*.

Source: thesun.co.uk

Abba's greatest hits compilation *Gold* has become the first record to spend

1000

weeks in the UK's album chart.

Source: bbc.co.uk

When I heard his voice in the headphones, I thought: 'Oh, I have to match this enormous, cool voice and the way he sings.' It's verrry sexy and a very good song.

Agnetha, on her duet with Gary Barlow, interview with Moira Petty, Daily Mail, 2013.

Source: dailymail.co.uk

Released in 2008,
Mamma Mia! the movie grossed
more than

$609m

worldwide.

66
We have talked about it, fantasised
like that. But we have done so
much, both of us now.
99

Agnetha, *on a reunion,* Attitude, *2013.*

Source: smh.com.au

It's the universality of the songs, people anywhere in the world can relate to them.

Benny, *on Abba's music, interview in* The Belfast Telegraph, *2017.*

Source: belfasttelgraph.co.uk

The collaboration between generations is extremely exciting.

Ash, *Avicii's Executive Producer, on collaboration between Benny, Bjorn and Avicii, 2013.*

The Adventures of Priscilla, Queen of the Desert and *Muriel's Wedding*, two Australian movies with Abba at their heart, were both released in

1994

We've made this journey throughout our history. Benny and Bjorn in particular. It's been very nostalgic.

Anni-Frid, *on playing together after 30 years, Expressen, 2016.*

Source: contactmusic.com

"

I think hearing Frida and Agnetha singing again is hard to beat. **"**

Benny, *on being back in the studio, 2021.*

Source: rollingstone.com

CHAPTER
FIVE

THE
VOYAGE
CONTINUES

After years of speculation,
the news was out:
new songs, a virtual tour and a
new album: Abba was back!

❝

I can't really explain it. It's tough.
There is a lot of technology
and a lot of light.

❞

Agnetha, *interview with Carolina Norén,*
Svensktoppens, 2021.

Source: newsbeezer.com

It's been a while since we made music together, almost 40 years, actually. We took a break in the spring of 1982 and now we've decided it's time to end it.

Abba, *official statement, 2021.*

Source: rollingstone.com

I don't feel that we have to prove anything. I don't feel we have to think about, 'Oh, what if it was better before?'

Benny, Chess *revival press night, 2018.*

Source: bbc.co.uk

"

So I called Frida and Agnetha and I said, 'What do you say, girls?' and they said 'yes' and I was a bit flabbergasted by that. "

Benny, *on the new material, interview with Zoe Ball, BBC Radio 2, 2021.*

Source: escbubble.com

You won't be able to see that they're not human beings.
It'll be spooky, I assure you, but great fun and no one has done it before.

Björn*, on the "Abba-tars", 2019.*

Source: smoothradio.com

I looked around and I looked into Agnetha's eyes and Frida's eyes and there was the same kind of feeling, the warmth and the friendship…

Björn, *interview with Zane Lowe, Apple Music, 2021.*

Source: nme.com

It was as if they'd just walked out
the door from 1979.

Ludvig Andersson (Benny's son), on the
band recording new music, interview with
Tom Bryant in The Mirror, 2021.

Source: mirror.co.uk

66

Anni-Frid and Agnetha's singing left everyone in the studio 'completely numb.'
They were just incredible.

99

Svana Gisla, *producer, on the band recording new music, interview with Tom Bryant in* The Mirror, *2021.*

Source: mirror.co.uk

So I say what I always say: I don't want to talk about money, politics and religion.

Agnetha, *on what she doesn't like to talk about, interviewed by Lasse Bengtsson, 2004.*

Source: abba-intermezzo.de

"

Oh my god, I'm such a big
Abba fan. When I saw that they
were coming back and they had
a record, I shot that link to
100 people I knew, then listened
to the new song and wept like
a baby.

"

Dave Grohl, BBC Breakfast, *2021*.

Source: bbc.co.uk

By the way, [if] the Abba reunion needs a fifth person! Hi, it can be me, I can do the backing vocals!

Alexandra Burke, Chess *revival press night, 2018.*

Source: bbc.co.uk

Voyage, the

2021

album, was the band's
first new music in over 40 years.

All these 40 years, we've been quite unanimous in not wanting to do something.

__Björn__, interview with Zane Lowe, Apple Music, 2021.

Source: nme.com

18- to 24-year-olds stream Abba the most on Spotify, and according to research, this particular demographic has been streaming more every year since 2014.

We create Abba in their prime –
1979 – as digital characters that we
will then use performance-capture
techniques to animate and
perform them and make them
look real.

Ben Morris, *Industrial Light & Magic, 2021.*

Abba had their first
top-10 hit in 40 years with
"Don't Shut Me Down"
in 2021.

The TikTok
#DancingQueenChallenge
had more than

160m

views in 2021.

66

Happiness only exists in the moment. Happiness is writing music.

99

Agnetha, *interview in VeckoRevyn, 1979.*

Source: agnetha-love.tumblr.com

Abba tribute band names
include
Björn Again,
Abba Mania
and
The Abba Tribute Band

66

My musical taste is very wide, but I do not listen to the likes of Lady Gaga and that sort of music much, I'm still playing music based on my past tastes. **99**

Anni-Frid, interview with Georg Cederskog, Dagens Nyheter, *2010.*

Source: icethesite.com

The idea of retirement is alien to me. When it gives you great joy to do something – in my case, make music – why on earth would you stop?

Benny, *interview in the* Belfast Telegraph, *2017.*

Source: belfasttelegraph.co.uk

"

Punk never got into my heart. You hear the anger now in rap, for example, but it's different and I like that very much. Eminem is one of my favourites.

"

Anni-Frid, The Guardian, *2014.*

Source: theguardian.com

I listened to this a lot when it came out, at a time when I wasn't writing pop songs any more.

Benny, *on Alanis Morissette's* Jagged Little Pill, *interview with Craig McLean in* The Guardian, *2009.*

Source: theguardian.com

Lily James sang really well [in *Mamma Mia 2*] – good singers make the job easier. Pierce Brosnan is good too. Everyone jokes that he's not very good but I think that's just because nobody wants to see James Bond in romantic scenes like that.

Benny, *interview on* Lorraine, *ITV, 2017.*

Source: digitalspy.com

Gold still conveys the one thing you absolutely need to know about the band: For about a decade, these four Swedes cracked the code on pop music.

Jamieson Cox, *Pitchfork review of* ABBA Gold: Greatest Hits, *2019.*

Source: pitchfork.com

"

Do they still sound like Abba?
Absolutely!

"

Tim de Lisle, Event Magazine,
Daily Mail, *2021.*

Source: dailymail.co.uk

We're not competing with Drake and all these other guys. We can't, because I don't understand the ingredients in the songs that work today.

Benny, *on Abba's new songs, 2021.*

"

I don't think we would want that actually, I certainly know myself I wouldn't want an actor – not while I'm alive – to play me on the big screen and I don't think the others would like that either.

"

Björn, *on the possibility of an Abba biopic,*
BBC Breakfast, *2021.*

Source: bbc.co.uk

We were simply starting to get out of touch with the pop music mainstream.

Björn, *"Do Abba's new songs live up to their hits?", Mark Savage, 2021.*

Source: bbc.co.uk

Abba were inducted
into the Rock and Roll
Hall of Fame in

2010

"Dancing Queen"
was inducted into the
Recording Academy's
Grammy Hall of Fame
in 2015.

My surname. You have no idea how many versions I've read and heard. It was especially irritating during my Abba years.

Björn, on what he would change, interview with Rosanna Greenstreet, The Guardian, 2020.

Source: theguardian.com

"

Being a songwriter myself and knowing what copyright has done for me and the sense of pride I have in owning my rights, I would tell any songwriter, 'Please don't do it unless you really, really have to.'

"

Björn, on copyright buyouts for songwriters, interview with Gadi Oron, Billboard, 2021.

Source: billboard.com

Billie Eilish is interesting. And of course I admire Taylor Swift as well. And Rihanna.

Benny, *on modern songwriters, interview with Ben Sisario in* The New York Times, *2021.*

Source: nytimes.com

> ❝
> I remember we were coming into Melbourne and there were people along the roads. There were thousands … because it was 'Moomba Day' not because of us, but we felt it was for us. ❞

Benny, *interview with Richard Wilkins, 2021.*

Source: smoothfm.com

Björn Again being named after me? It's pretty cool. Whenever I have to call people back I say 'it's Björn again'.

Björn, *2009.*

Source: bjornagain.com

Anni-Frid was born in Norway,
to a Norwegian mother and
German father, and her marriage
to a prince in 1992 makes her
full, formal name
"Princess Anni-Frid, Dowager
Countess of Plauen".

There will be new music this year, that's for sure.

Björn, The Herald Sun, *2021*.

Source: netherlandsnewslive.com

66

We could sing 'The Way Old Folks Do'.

99

Björn, *on the possibility of a reunion, 2010.*

Source: independent.ie

Why should we do it? We have done so many songs, during such a long time. The fact that we had two divorces, and there was no meaning, I think, with getting together, again.

Agnetha, *on a reunion, 2011.*

Source: bbc.co.uk

I've learned never to say never.
You just don't know. But I've
reached an age when you start
taking it easier. But I enjoy singing.
I still sing – at home. **"**

Anni-Frid, *on a comeback, interview with*
Fredrik Skavlan, 2014.

CHAPTER
SIX

THANK YOU FOR THE MUSIC

Abba's main album releases
and the songs on them.

Ring Ring
(1973)

Ring Ring
Another Town, Another Train
Disillusion
People Need Love
I Saw It in the Mirror
Nina, Pretty Ballerina
Love Isn't Easy (But It Sure Is Hard
Enough)
Me and Bobby and Bobby's Brother
He Is Your Brother
She's My Kind of Girl
I Am Just A Girl
Rock 'N Roll Band

Waterloo

(1974)

Waterloo
Sitting in the Palmtree
King Kong Song
Hasta Mañana
My Mama Said
Dance (While the Music Still Goes On)
Honey, Honey
Watch Out
What About Livingstone?
Gonna Sing You My Lovesong
Suzy-Hang-Around
Ring Ring

ABBA
(1975)

Mamma Mia
Hey, Hey Helen
Tropical Loveland
SOS
Man in the Middle
Bang-A-Boomerang
I Do, I Do, I Do, I Do, I Do
Rock Me
Intermezzo No. 1
I've Been Waiting For You
So Long

Arrival

(1976)

When I Kissed the Teacher
Dancing Queen
My Love, My Life
Dum Dum Diddle
Knowing Me, Knowing You
Money, Money, Money
That's Me
Why Did It Have to Be Me?
Tiger
Arrival

ABBA: The Album
(1977)

Eagle

Take A Chance on Me

One Man, One Woman

The Name of the Game

Move On

Hole In Your Soul

The Girl With the Golden Hair (Three scenes from a mini-musical)

Thank You For the Music

I Wonder (Departure)

I'm a Marionette

Voulez-Vous

(1979)

As Good As New
Voulez-Vous
I Have a Dream
Angeleyes
The King Has Lost His Crown
Does Your Mother Know
If It Wasn't for the Nights
Chiqitita
Lovers (Live a Little Longer)
Kisses of Fire

Super Trouper
(1980)

Super Trouper
The Winner Takes It All
On and On and On
Andante, Andante
Me and I
Happy New Year
Our Last Summer
The Piper
Lay All Your Love on Me
The Way Old Friends Do (live)

The Visitors

(1981)

The Visitors
Head Over Heels
When All is Said and Done
Soldiers
I Let the Music Speak
One of Us
Two for the Price of One
Slipping Through My Fingers
Like an Angel Passing Through My
    Room

ABBA Gold (1992)

Dancing Queen
Knowing Me, Knowing You
Take a Chance on Me
Mamma Mia
Lay All Your Love on Me
Super Trouper
I Have a Dream
The Winner Takes It All
Money, Money, Money
SOS
Chiquitita
Fernando
Voulez-Vous
Gimme! Gimme! Gimme! (A Man
    After Midnight)
Does Your Mother Know

One of Us
The Name of the Game
Thank You For the Music
Waterloo

Voyage (2021)

I Still Have Faith In You
When You Dance With Me
Little Things
Don't Shut Me Down
Just a Notion
I Can Be That Woman
Keep an Eye on Dan
Bumblebee
No Doubt About It
Ode to Freedom

Abba was formed out of love, you could say. Björn and I were in love. And so were Benny and Anni-Frid.

Agnetha *interview in* VeckoRevyn, *1979.*

Source: agnetha-love.tumblr.com